AROUND ONE LOG

Chipmunks, Spiders, and Creepy Insiders

By Anthony D. Fredericks

Illustrated by Jennifer DiRubbio

Dawn Publications

To the memory of my father, James B. Fredericks, who introduced me to rainbow trout, alpine trails, rotting logs and lifelong lessons deep in the majestic Sierra Nevada Mountains. — ADF

To my husband Rob, for your overwhelming support, your encouraging critiques, and for all your sacrifices. I wouldn't be where I am now but for you. — JDR

Library of Congress Cataloging-in-Publication Data
Fredericks, Anthony D.
  Around one log : chipmunks, spiders, and creepy insiders / by Anthony D. Fredericks ;
illustrated by Jennifer DiRubbio. -- 1st ed.
    p. cm.
  ISBN 978-1-58469-137-2 (hardback) -- ISBN 978-1-58469-138-9 (pbk.) 1. Forest animals--
Habitations--Juvenile literature. 2. Dead trees--Ecology--Juvenile literature. 3. Biodegradation--
Juvenile literature. I. DiRubbio, Jennifer. II. Title.
  QL112.F733 2011
  591.73--dc22
                                                2010031037

Dawn Publications
12402 Bitney Springs Road
Nevada City, CA 95959
530-274-7775
nature@dawnpub.com

Manufactured by Regent Publishing Services, Hong Kong
Printed January, 2011, in ShenZhen, Guangdong, China

10 9 8 7 6 5 4 3 2 1
First Edition

Design and computer production by Patty Arnold, Menagerie Design and Publishing

Dear Visitors:

I live in a great place—a rotting log! This log is an *important* place because it's *home*. Just like yours. Well, maybe not exactly . . . but it provides food, somewhere to sleep, and a place to get out of the rain and snow. Us roly-polies like to eat good stuff like dead leaves, rotting wood, and animal poop—yum! People call it a "habitat."

This old log is also great entertainment! I have lots of weird neighbors, and remember, weird is interesting. Some of our neighbors are predators (they hunt other animals), and some of them are prey (the hunted). Some hang around for a long time, while others just come and go. Some are huge, but friendly, like the chipmunk. Others are often hungry, like daddy longlegs. Whenever we see them, it's time to roll up in a ball.

Us roly-polies like to be up and around when it's nice and cool and dark. Some of our neighbors insist on being up and around during the day. It takes all kinds! But whether friend or foe, we all like our wonderful habitat—our log.

We hope you enjoy visiting our home . . . our rot-rotting log!

Your balled-up buddy,

Roly - poly

Here stood a great tree with branches high.
  It flourished and grew—up toward the sky.
But a summer storm and a lightning stroke
  Splintered the wood in this giant oak.
Then a muscled wind blew all around
  And the ancient tree tumbled to the ground.

This was the **tree**.

Long soaking rains seeped into some spaces;
Wide patches of moss spread over these places.
Over time the great tree slowly wasted away—
The once mighty trunk began to decay.

Then ants, worms, and millipedes prowled here and there,
While crickets and beetles dashed everywhere.
All through the years this rotting **log** site
Was a home for critters, both day and night.

These are the **termites** that feed on the wood.
　　They chew and devour—to them it tastes good!
From top to bottom, inside and out,
　　Both friend and foe all ramble about.

A quick **salamander** scared by a sound
　　Darts 'neath the log and soft squishy ground.
He's a neighbor to termites that feed on the wood.
　　They chew and devour—to them it tastes good!
From top to bottom, inside and out,
　　Both friend and foe all ramble about.

Some gray **roly-polies**, rounded and small,
Hide deep inside tunnels, curled into a ball.
It's their home near the salamander scared by a sound
Who darts 'neath the log and the soft squishy ground.

He's a neighbor to termites that feed on the wood.
They chew and devour—to them it tastes good!
From top to bottom, inside and out,
Both friend and foe all ramble about.

A sole **garter snake** in search of some prey
  Slithers and slides for most of the day,
Above roly-polies, rounded and small,
  Hidden deep inside tunnels, curled into a ball.
It's their home near the salamander scared by a sound
  Who darts 'neath the log and the soft squishy ground.
He's a neighbor to termites that feed on the wood.
  They chew and devour—to them it tastes good!
From top to bottom, inside and out,
  Both friend and foe all ramble about.

These red **velvet mites**—a hundred or so—
　Swarm over the log, on top and below.
They live with the snake in search of some prey
　Who slithers and slides for most of the day,
Above roly-polies, rounded and small,
　Hidden deep inside tunnels, curled into a ball.
It's their home near the salamander scared by a sound
　Who darts 'neath the log and the soft squishy ground.
He's a neighbor to termites that feed on the wood.
　They chew and devour—to them it tastes good!
From top to bottom, inside and out,
　Both friend and foe all ramble about.

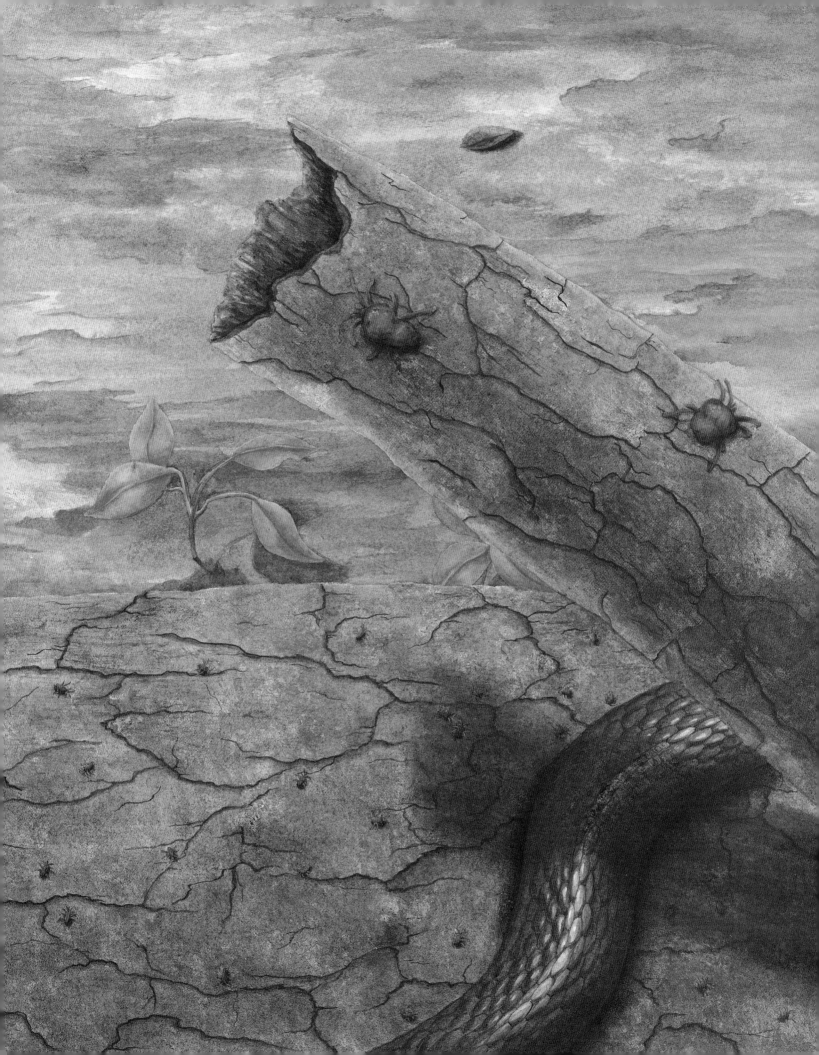

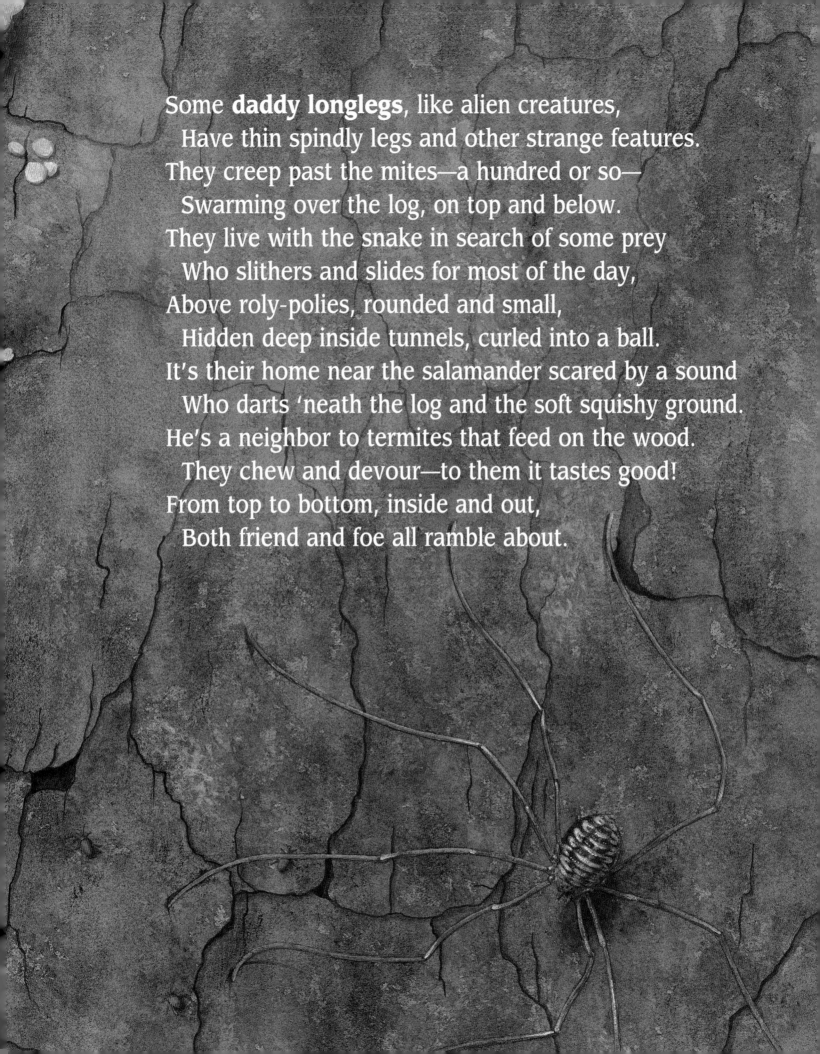

Some **daddy longlegs**, like alien creatures,
  Have thin spindly legs and other strange features.
They creep past the mites—a hundred or so—
  Swarming over the log, on top and below.
They live with the snake in search of some prey
  Who slithers and slides for most of the day,
Above roly-polies, rounded and small,
  Hidden deep inside tunnels, curled into a ball.
It's their home near the salamander scared by a sound
  Who darts 'neath the log and the soft squishy ground.
He's a neighbor to termites that feed on the wood.
  They chew and devour—to them it tastes good!
From top to bottom, inside and out,
  Both friend and foe all ramble about.

This is the **chipmunk** who twitters and squeaks,
  Then gathers some seeds and packs up her cheeks.
She springs over longlegs, those alien creatures,
  With their spindly legs and other strange features.
They creep past the mites—a hundred or so—
  Swarming over the log, on top and below.
They live with the snake in search of some prey
  Who slithers and slides for most of the day,
Above roly-polies, rounded and small,
  Hidden deep inside tunnels, curled into a ball.
It's their home near the salamander scared by a sound
  Who darts 'neath the log and the soft squishy ground.
He's a neighbor to termites that feed on the wood.
  They chew and devour—to them it tastes good!
From top to bottom, inside and out,
  Both friend and foe all ramble about.

Year after year the log continued to rot.
Then a class on a walk came up to this spot.
One student—she asked, to her teacher she said—
"Is this log alive? Or is it now dead?"

Somewhere, some place, a wild summer storm thunders and crashes through a forest of oak trees. An old tree, standing tall, is struck by lightning. A strong gust of wind pushes and shoves its way across the forest. The tree, weakened and cracked, tumbles to the ground. Timber!

Oak Tree

Oak is a universal symbol of strength and endurance. Oak trees can be found throughout the world—in fact, there are about 600 different species, with eighty of those species living in North America. All oaks are deciduous (they lose their leaves in the fall) and all of them have a fruit known as an acorn. Throughout the centuries oak wood has been used to build homes, create beautiful furniture, or construct sailing ships. Oaks have been chosen as the national tree of many countries including the United States, England, France, Germany, Poland, and Bulgaria, among others.

Fantastic Fact: The Pechanga Great Oak Tree, in Temecula, California, is the oldest oak tree in the United States (and perhaps the world). It is at least 2,000 years old.

Termites

Termites have been around ever since the time of the dinosaurs. Most species feed on wood, which they digest with the help of tiny organisms that live in their intestines. Termites can cause serious structural damage to wooden buildings. Most species of termites live in large colonies which may have anywhere from several hundred to several million individuals. A termite colony is composed of nymphs (semi-mature young), workers, soldiers, and one or more queens, each of whom can produce millions of eggs. There are about 2,100 different species of termites throughout the world, including 41 in North America.

Fantastic Fact: In Africa, a few species of termites build large earthen mounds throughout the tropical savanna. Some of these mounds may be 30 feet high—the height of five adults standing one on top of the other.

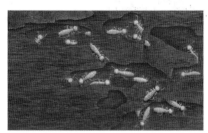

Salamander

Although they look like lizards, salamanders are more closely related to frogs and toads. Normally nocturnal and voiceless, they lack the scaly skin and claws of lizards. Most salamander species live near brooks, creeks, streams, and other moist areas. There are about 500 species of salamanders throughout the world, with about 150 species in North America. The smallest salamander in the world is the Minute Salamander which grows to a length of just over one inch (including the tail). The Chinese Giant salamander, on the other hand, grows to six feet in length and weighs up to 140 pounds.

Fantastic Fact: Salamanders can regenerate (re-grow) lost limbs and other injured body parts.

Roly-poly

Roly-polies are a type of wood lice. They have the unique ability to roll themselves up into a ball whenever danger is near. When roly-polies feel the vibrations of an approaching enemy they pull in their feet and quickly gather themselves into a spheroid. In this way they are similar to armadillos, found throughout the southern United States—another animal that can roll itself up into a ball for protection. Roly-polies are usually found in damp, dark places such as under rocks and logs. They are nocturnal (awake during the night) and feed mostly on dead plant matter. Most roly-polies have eleven body segments with one pair of legs in each segment.

Fantastic Fact: In some parts of the United States a roly-poly is called a "doodle bug" or a "pill bug." But they aren't insects at all—they're isopods, segmented creatures closely related to crabs and lobsters.

Months later, the trunk of the tree looks quiet and still. But look closely and you'll see some movement—bugs are skipping here and there, lizards are scooting about, and tiny creatures are slipping in and out of the slowly rotting wood. Some will stay for a long time, others are just passing through. For each of these creatures the old tree has become a new home—it has taken on new life.

Garter Snake

Garter snakes live throughout North America from Alaska (it's the only species of snake found in Alaska) all the way to Central America. According to several scientists, it may be the most widely distributed reptile in North America. In very cold regions large groups of these snakes—consisting of thousands of members—will often hibernate together. After mating, a female may give birth to as many as 80 babies at one time. Garter snakes eat a variety of animals such as earthworms, insects, lizards, spiders, fish, birds, and slugs. Their major enemies include hawks, raccoons, crows, and crayfish. They are not dangerous to humans.

Fantastic Fact: Some species of garter snakes will constrict (wrap themselves around and squeeze) small mammals. In many ways, they are a miniature equivalent of a python.

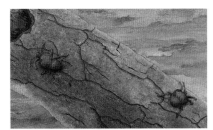

Velvet Mites

Known for their bright red colors, adult red velvet mites are capable of attacking and consuming prey many times their size. As a result they help keep the insect population in check. These tiny creatures—just 1/8" long—spend most of their lives scurrying over the forest floor, scampering through leaf litter, or crawling over and under old logs and branches. Young mites are frequently parasites, riding on other creatures such as grasshoppers, locusts, and crickets. Their bodies, typically oval in shape, are covered with a coat of fine red hairs, making them appear hairy and velvety.

Fantastic Fact: When it comes into contact with a potential predator, a red velvet mite will quickly fold up all its legs.

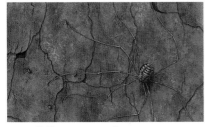

Daddy Longlegs

These creatures, often known as "harvestmen," look like spiders with four pairs of extremely long legs. However, they are not spiders. Spiders have two separate body parts and eight eyes; Daddy Longlegs have one body part and just two eyes. There are over 200 species in North America. They are known for their exceptionally long walking legs which, in one species, can be six inches or more. If disturbed, they furiously wave the second pair of legs in the air. Some daddy longlegs eat tiny animals and plant materials, while others are scavengers, eating only dead organisms.

Fantastic Fact: If a daddy longlegs is attacked and a leg is broken off, that leg will continue to twitch, sometimes for up to an hour. With luck, the predator watches the jerking limb while the daddy longlegs escapes.

Chipmunk

You may have seen these black-striped creatures scampering over the forest floor or darting up the trunk of a tree. Chipmunks range throughout North America and typically live on a varied diet including nuts, seeds, fruits, berries, bird's eggs, worms, small frogs, and insects. At the beginning of autumn chipmunks gather lots of food items and store them near their nests for winter. Most chipmunks live in long underground burrows, although some will build nests in the hollow limb of a tree. Their burrows can be up to ten feet long with one or more entrances. Most chipmunks are very vocal—you may have heard one or more chattering, chirping, or twittering.

Fantastic Fact: The home range of a chipmunk may be up to 1/2 acre, but the adult only defends a territory of about 50 feet around the burrow entrance.

Activities, Projects, and Lots of Cool Ideas!

I hope you had fun reading this book . . . I sure had fun writing it! If you'd like to learn more about rotting logs and the animals that live there, here are some cool activities. Some of these you can do yourself; others may require adult help. Choose the ones you like and be sure to share what you learn with others.

A Day in My Life

Select one of the animals in the book. Visit your school library or public library to learn more about your chosen animal. Then write a series of diary entries as told from the perspective of the creature. For example, "A Day in the Life of a Roly-poly," or "My Life as a Daddy Longlegs," or "One Hour with a Garter Snake."

All Year Long

Find an old log near where you live. Take photographs of the log throughout the year (once a week, for example) and maintain a diary or journal of the events or changes that take place around the log. What animals come to visit the log? What does the log look like when it rains, snows, or is sunny outside? Who lives there all the time?

Read Some More

You may enjoy reading other books I've written (and were illustrated by my friend, Jennifer DiRubbio) about other fascinating communities of animals. See page 32 for their titles.

Readers Theatre

You can turn part of this book into a readers theatre script! I have written lots of readers theatre books for teachers. Your teacher can check them out at www.teacherideaspress.com. Below you will see how I took the first part of the story and turned it into a readers theatre script . . . but I didn't finish it! Work with a friend to complete this script and then share it with others.

ALEX: Hey look, there's a big tree on the ground.

BONNIE: Yeah, it must have fallen in a storm a long time ago.

CARL: Look at all the moss.

DAVID: It's also starting to decay in different places.

ELLEN: Hey guys, look at this, there's ants, worms and millipedes.

ALEX: And, I see some crickets and beetles.

BONNIE: Hey, look at the termites!

CARL: Yuck! I can't believe they really like to eat all that wood.

DAVID: Shhhh, there's a little salamander over there.

ELLEN: I think he's one of the neighbors for the termites.

[Now, how would you like to write the rest of this story?]

Seek and Search

Ask an adult for an assortment of old magazines (such as National Geographic, Ranger Rick, National Wildlife), particularly ones that have pictures of animals in them. Cut out pictures of animals that you might find in and around a rotting log. Use some glue or paste and make a picture collage of all the animals that might live around a rotting log. You may want to post this collage in your room at home or share it with your classmates at school.

Read This Book

Create a poster or advertisement that will encourage other kids to read this book. What information, data, or illustrations should be included? You may wish to hang your poster in the classroom, the hallway, or the school library.

LOOK AND SEE

Ask an adult to take you to a place where there is a rotting log. Sit down on the ground and quietly watch the log for about 15 to 20 minutes (make sure the adult is quiet, too). What do you see? What do you hear? What are some things going on in and around the log? Take some time to share what you learn with the adult.

FOR RENT

Look through the classified section of your local newspaper. Based on examples in the newspaper, create an original classified advertisement based on information in the book. Here's one I wrote:

FOR RENT: One rotting log. Sometimes wet, sometimes dry. Lots of neighbors and lots of visitors. Great views of the forest. Reasonable rates. Available immediately. Call Daddy Longlegs at 123-4567 any time before nightfall.

FIND OUT MORE

You may wish to log onto one or more of the following web sites:

National Wildlife Federation: http://www.nwf.org/wildlife/

eNature: http://www.enature.com/home/

Electronic Zoo: http://netvet.wustl.edu/e-zoo.htm

Animal Diversity Web: http://animaldiversity.ummz.umich.edu/site/index.html

You may wish to locate various animals profiled in this book. What new information can you discover about some of these creatures? How could you share that information with your classmates? With a poster? brochure? flyer?

FINGER PLAY

Cut off the "fingers" from an inexpensive pair of work gloves (ask an adult to help you). Use some art materials such as crayons, yarn, felt-tip pens, and sequins to turn each "finger" into a puppet representing one of the creatures in the book. You may want to retell the story to a friend or adult using your miniature animal puppets.

WRITE ON!

The book begins with a letter from "your balled-up buddy," the roly-poly. You may wish to create other possible introductory letters for the book using one or more of the featured animals as narrator(s). What would a letter from the garter snake say? What would a letter from the chipmunk sound like? Be sure to share the letter(s) with other students.

DICTIONARY

You may enjoy creating a "Rotting Log Dictionary." Read other books, visit the Internet, talk with adults, and gather words or terms that could be used in the dictionary. I came up with a few ideas to get you started:

A = Ants, Animals

B = Bugs, Bark

C = Critters, Chipmunk

D = Damp, Dead Leaves

E = Environment, Eat.

JUST MAKE ME!

You may wish to create some of the animals in this book using your own homemade clay. Ask an adult to help you with the following recipe: Mix one cup of flour and 1/2 cup of salt. Add 1/3 cup of water, a little at a time. Squeeze the dough until it is smooth. Form it into shapes and let it air dry for 2-3 days (or bake it in an oven at 225 degrees for about 30 minutes). Paint the dry shape with tempera paints.

Anthony D. Fredericks grew up in southern California and spent his summers hiking and fishing the majestic Sierra Nevadas. Now Tony explores the mountainside in south-central Pennsylvania where he and his wife live. A former classroom teacher and reading specialist, he is Professor of Education at York College, York, PA. He is the author of more than three dozen children's books.

Jennifer DiRubbio is both a passionate artist and an avid environmentalist. She has been active as an artist for several organizations that promote nature and a healthy planet. Jennifer graduated with a BFA from Pratt Institute in 1992. She keeps her home and studio in Merrick, New York, as "green" and environmentally sound as possible, where her husband and two young children also work and play.

OTHER BOOKS BY ANTHONY FREDERICKS AND JENNIFER DIRUBBIO

Under One Rock: Bugs, Slugs and Other Ughs — A whole community of creatures lives under rocks. No child will be able to resist taking a peek after reading this.

In One Tidepool: Crabs, Snails and Salty Tails — Have you ever ventured to the edge of the sea and peered into a tidepool? A colorful community of creatures lives there!

Around One Cactus: Owls, Bats and Leaping Rats — A saguaro cactus may look lonely, standing in the dry, dry desert—but it is a haven for creatures, both cute and creepy!

Near One Cattail: Turtles, Logs and Leaping Frogs — What creatures live in a bog-boggy place? Many. And they swim, crawl, and soar!

On One Flower: Butterflies, Ticks and a Few More Icks — Two boys discover an array of amazing critters when they stop and really look at a goldenrod flower.

A FEW OTHER AWARD-WINNING BOOKS FROM DAWN

Over in the Ocean, Over in the Jungle, Over in the Arctic, and *Over in Australia* — Children will want to sing, clap, and count along as they learn about remarkable creatures that inhabit these fascinating places.

The BLUES Go Birding series features a unique team of bluebirds that are crazy about bird-watching! Their delightful antics will introduce a new generation to the wonderful sport of birding.

    The BLUES Go Birding Across America
    The BLUES Go Birding at Wild America's Shores
    The BLUES Go Extreme Birding

In the Trees, Honey Bees — A remarkable inside-the-hive view of a wild colony of honey bees, along with simple rhymes and solid information, make this a favorite among bee-lovers.

Dawn Publications is dedicated to inspiring in children a deeper understanding and appreciation for all life on Earth. To view our titles or to order, visit us at www.dawnpub.com or call 800-545-7475.